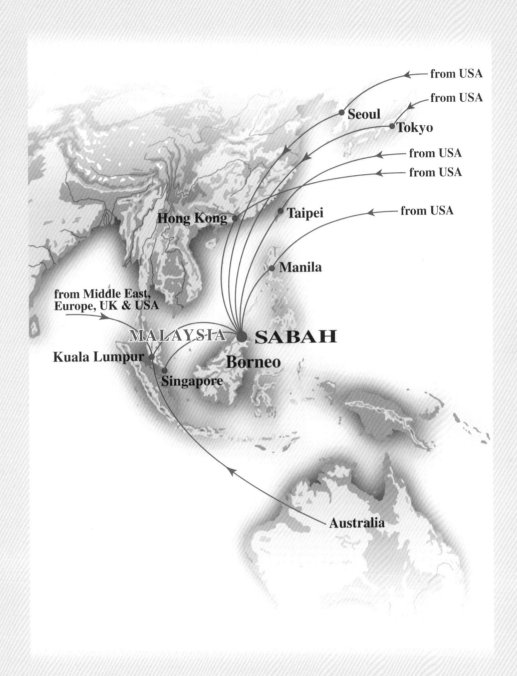

from USA

from USA

from USA

from USA

from USA

Seoul

Tokyo

Hong Kong

Taipei

Manila

from Middle East,
Europe, UK & USA

MALAYSIA

SABAH

Kuala Lumpur

Borneo

Singapore

Australia

Discovering Sabah

C.L. Chan

Discovering Sabah

Natural History Publications (Borneo)
Kota Kinabalu

2002

Published by

NATURAL HISTORY PUBLICATIONS (BORNEO) SDN. BHD.

(Company No. 216807-X)
A913, 9th Floor, Phase 1, Wisma Merdeka
P.O. Box 15566
88864 Kota Kinabalu, Sabah, Malaysia
Tel: 6088-233098 Fax: 6088-240768
e-mail: chewlun@tm.net.my
http://www.nhpborneo.com

First published 2001.
Reprinted April 2002.

Discovering Sabah

Text by Wendy Hutton

Photographs by Tengku D.Z. Adlin, Au Kam Wah, C.L. Chan, Tommy Chang/Sabah Tourism Promotion Corporation, Joseph Charles, Chin Shui Hiung, Charles Clarke, Indraniel Das, Simon Enderby/Scubazoo Images, Andrea e Antonella Ferrari, David Goh, Wendy Hutton, Jason Isley/Scubazoo Images, Susan K. Jacobson, Jones/Shimlock, Anthony Lamb, Lim Chan Koon, S.P. Lim, Loi Pui King, Anthea Phillipps, W.M. Poon, Cede Prudente, Sabah Air, Sabah Wildlife Department, Francis Seow-Choen, Sualim Takun, William Tan, Tee Kim Ling, Tham Yau Kong, Wong Khoon Meng, Michael Patrick Wong, WWF/Tan Hui Shim, and Yong Lee Ming

Design and layout by C.L. Chan and Cheng Jen Wai

Perpustakaan Negara Malaysia Cataloguing-in-Publication Data

Hutton, Wendy
    Discovering Sabah / text by Wendy Hutton ; photographs
    by Tengku D. Z. Adlin ... [et al] ; paintings by Yong Ket
    Hyun ; foreword by Datuk Chong Kah Kiat.
    ISBN 983-812-046-4
    1. Sabah—Description and travel. I. Tengku D. Z. Adlin.
    II. Yong, Ket Hyun. III. Chong, Kah Kiat, Datuk.
    915.9521

Printed in Malaysia.

Contents

C.L. Chan

C.L. Chan

Foreword

by

Datuk Chong Kah Kiat, J.P.

Chief Minister
and
Minister of Tourism, Environment, Science and Technology,
Sabah

Sabah, at the northern tip of the world's third largest island, offers astonishing variety within its relatively small size. There are superb white sandy beaches and coral islands, some of them world famous as diving locations, and across its fertile plains, intriguing wetlands and rain forests, there exists also a wondrous range of plants and animals, culminating in the treasures of Mount Kinabalu, the highest mountain between the Himalayas and New Guinea and a World Heritage Site. Sabah is, quite simply, stunning.

Despite its unique attractions and well developed tourism infrastructure, Sabah has only recently become known to discerning travellers. They are invariably surprised by all that Sabah has to offer, and at the easy accessibility of places that might, in other parts of the world, require mounting a major expedition to explore. Visitors can, for example, watch orang-utans in a rain forest sanctuary, see giant sea turtles come ashore to lay their eggs, snorkel or scuba dive over reefs, explore a cave where edible bird's nests have been gathered for centuries, travel by boat through Malaysia's largest wetlands area to view Borneo's unique proboscis monkey—all this within a couple of hours or less of an airport and luxurious accommodation.

You might begin your discovery of Sabah through the pages of this book, now in its second edition. Here is your introduction to the fascinating land and people of Sabah.

Datuk Chong Kah Kiat, J.P.
March 2002

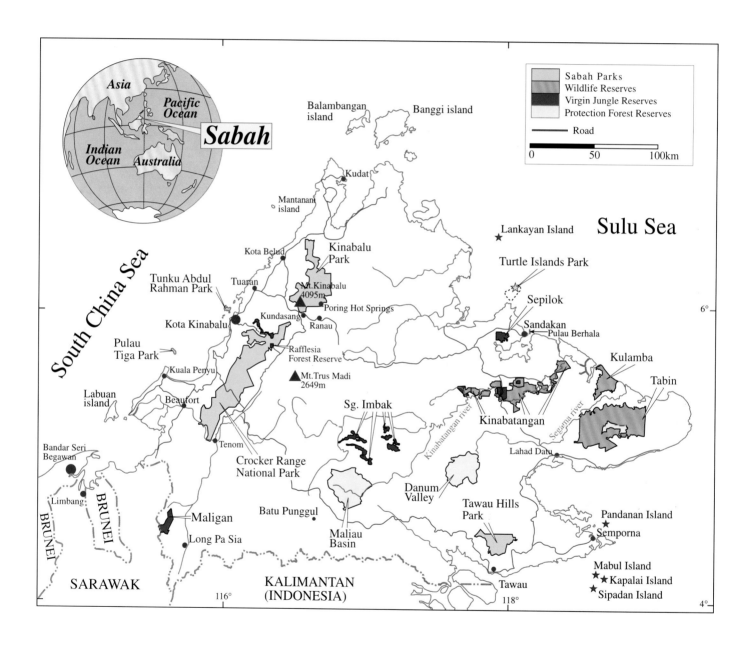

Chapter 1

Introduction

Surprisingly for a land offering so many superlative attractions, Sabah remains almost as much of a mystery to the outside world as it was during the 18th and 19th centuries, when explorers believed that Borneo was inhabited by men with tails.

Spread across the northern tip of one of the world's largest islands, Sabah seems almost unfairly blessed with natural beauty. With its magnificent rain forests, rugged mountainous interior, idyllic islands and beaches, it encapsulates the very best of Borneo. Despite being part of a fast-modernising

Wendy Hutton

Opposite: Sabah occupies the northern tip of Borneo, the world's third largest island. **Left:** A canoe with bamboo outriggers sails in Darvel Bay, off Semporna, departure point for world-class scuba diving sites off the southeast coast.

Jones/Shimlock

C.L. Chan

Above and right: Green Turtles, an endangered species, are found in Sabah waters, particularly off the east coast. At the Turtle Islands Park north of Sandakan, eggs laid by turtles coming ashore are protected. The hatchlings are released into the sea and in about twenty years, those that survive will return to mate at the island where they were hatched.

C.L. Chan

Left: A Kadazandusun girl, in traditional dress, holds a popular musical instrument known as a *sompoton.* Made of reeds and a dried gourd, it produces a haunting sound; many visitors find that it also makes an attractive souvenir.

nation, Sabah (one of the 13 states which formed the Federation of Malaysia in 1963) still retains a simplicity and charm, due largely to its remarkably warm and welcoming people.

Sabah is relatively small, just 75,000 square kilometres or one-tenth of the total land area of Borneo, yet its borders encompass an astonishing diversity of peoples, landscapes, plants and animals. The terrain ranges from long white sandy beaches to coastal mangroves, from vast freshwater swamps to fertile coastal plains, from limestone caves to ranges covered with rain forest, all this culminating in the stunning granite peak of Mount Kinabalu, the highest mountain between the Himalayas and New Guinea. Lying off Sabah's almost 1,500 kilometres of coastline are coral reefs teeming with marine life, and islands which might have been created to fulfill the dream of a tropical island paradise.

The rich variety of plant life, with everything from the world's largest flower to orchids so tiny they can scarcely be seen with the naked eye, is a source of constant delight. And Sabah's rainbow of birds and its even more remarkable mammals, including the gentle orang-utan and almost grotesque proboscis monkey, are surprisingly accessible.

Begin your discovery of Sabah as you turn these pages.

Joseph Charles

C.L. Chan

Wendy Hutton

Above: Sabah's butterflies include this Common Birdwing and its equally striking cousin, Rajah Brooke's Birdwing.
Left: The seeds of a palm tree make a striking contrast to the gloom of the rain forest, where the canopy limits the amount of light reaching the forest floor. **Opposite:** It is easy to see how the proboscis monkey got its name. The male, with its huge, pendulous nose and pot belly, is one of the most remarkable sights awaiting visitors to the Kinabatangan River, on the east coast.

5

Tee Kim Ling

Cede Prudente

C.L. Chan

Opposite above: Kota Kinabalu, Sabah's capital. The first British settlement on the west coast was located on Pulau Gaya. It was moved to its present location after the original village was burned by a Bajau rebel, Mat Salleh, in 1897. **Opposite below:** Bajau children.

Wendy Hutton

C.L. Chan

Left above: Nepenthes, more commonly known as pitcher plants, are found in Kinabalu Park. This giant specimen, *Nepenthes rajah*, the world's largest pitcher plant, is found only on Mt Kinabalu and Mt Tamboyukon. **Left below:** The winsome face of a baby orang-utan. These gentle apes, found only in Borneo and Sumatra, still live in the rain forests of Sabah. They can more easily be seen at the Sepilok Orang-utan Rehabilitation Sanctuary near Sandakan, and in a sanctuary at a Pantai Dalit resort. **Above:** Murut dancers doing the fast-moving bamboo dance, popular during longhouse celebrations and at cultural performances.

Tommy Chang/STPC

Above: It used to be said that the only time nomadic sea gypsies—who once lived aboard their boats off Sabah's east coast—came ashore was after they died. Old carved grave markers can still be found on some of the islands off Semporna. **Right:** A rhododendron found growing in dry heath forest (*kerangas*) of the remote Maliau Basin. **Opposite:** The rituals of the Kadazandusun priestesses or *bobohizan* have been passed down over the centuries.

W.M. Poon

W.M. Poon

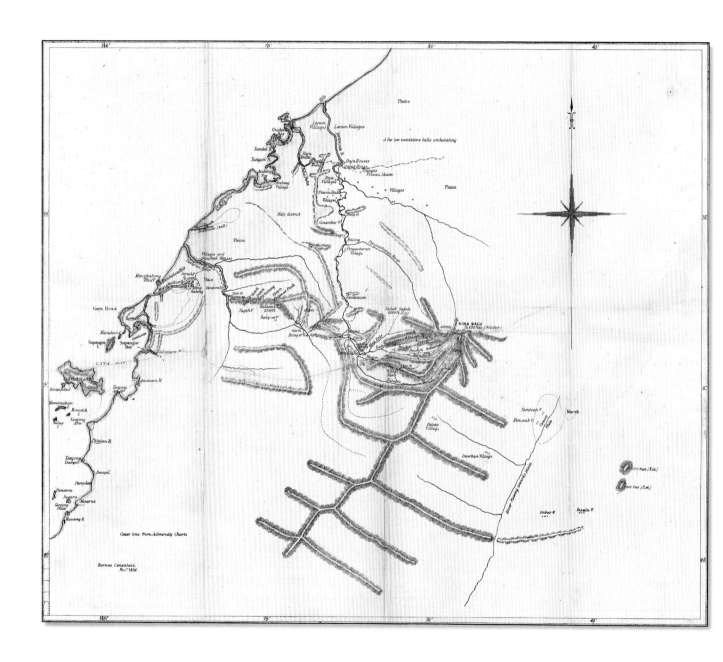

Chapter 2

In the Beginning

Borneo—an island that seems filled with timeless mystery—is in fact relatively young from a geological point of view. The basis of the island was first laid down by the buckling of the earth's crust around 15 million years ago. Movement of the earth's tectonic plates some three million years ago—long after the age of dinosaurs—forced these layers of limestone, sandstone and mudstone to rise up from the bottom of the ocean and form what is now Borneo. Until the last Ice Age, Borneo was linked with

Opposite: A map printed in 1858 shows the west coast of Sabah, with Gaya Island seen to the far left, and the Crocker Range dominated by Mount Kinabalu shown in the centre. **Left:** A view of Mt Kinabalu (seen from the west) from Carl Bock's sensational book, *The Head-Hunters of Borneo.*

Discovering Sabah

Java, Sumatra and the Malay peninsula to form the huge land mass known as Sundaland. When the ice cap melted some 12,000 years ago, sea levels rose and Borneo was isolated to become the world's third largest island.

Below: Kota Kinabalu (formerly known as Jesselton) with Pulau Sepangar seen in the background, January 1911.

The beginnings of Sabah's people lie far back in the realms of pre-history. Archaeological excavations around the bed of an ancient lake at Tingkayu, in eastern Sabah, unearthed evidence of men living here as long as 20,000 years ago. What happened to these earliest Sabahans, who made relatively

Sabah Museum

12

Wendy Hutton

Left: A string of trophies taken by a famous head-hunter of North Borneo, Monsopiad. The taking of heads was not a random act but part of complex ritual.

sophisticated flaked stone tools, remains a mystery. The forebearers of today's indigenous tribes were Austronesians who began arriving from the north around 2,500 BC. By this time, the people who had lived around Lake Tingkayu had long disappeared, and today, none of the tribes in Sabah (or, indeed, anywhere in Borneo) speak pre-Austronesia languages.

Before the 10th century AD, Chinese traders began voyaging south in search of Borneo's treasures, exchanging large ceramic storage jars and other items for such exotica as edible birds' nests, medicinal products from the jungle, damar resin, rattan and hornbill casques to make the "golden jade" highly prized by China's emperors. According to Brunei historical records, a Chinese settlement existed on the east coast of Sabah along the Kinabatangan River during the 14th century.

Sabah was, by this time, under the nominal control of the Sultan of Brunei, who ruled over much of north Borneo until the 19th century. Owing to the proximity of the rich northeast coast of Sabah to the Sulu islands of the southern Philippines, the Sultan of Sulu made an attempt to gain control of this region during the 17th century. The Sultan of Brunei failed to honour a verbal agreement to cede Sabah to Sulu, a promise made during internal battles for succession in Brunei, so it remained within Brunei's domain. It is doubtful, however, that the indigenous people living in Sabah's scattered

Sabah Museum

Above & opposite:
Murut tribesmen photographed in the early days of British North Borneo *c.* 1909.

coastal and riverine communities either knew or cared about such political matters.

Sabah today has the greatest diversity of ethnic groups in all of Malaysia. The different tribal groups can, however, be grouped into four major linguistic families: Dusunic, Murutic, Paitanic and Tidong. The indigenous Sabahans were joined by Muslim settlers, who came from the islands of the southern Philippines in the 18th and 19th centuries. With the arrival of these newcomers—Bajau, Irranun, Obian, Suluk and Tausug—many of the indigenous coastal dwellers moved inland, across the mountainous terrain dividing the west coast from the fertile interior plains, joining other indigenous tribes already inhabiting the hinterland.

Sabah Museum

During a period of colonial expansion in the 19th century, various Westerners turned their attention towards Sabah. An Austrian, Baron Von Overbeck, bought the rights to Sabah from the Sultan of Brunei, and, just to be on the safe side, also paid the Sultan of Sulu, who exerted considerable influence over trade along the northeast coast. Von Overbeck, together with Englishman Alfred Dent, established the British North Borneo Chartered Company in 1882. This company, with the protection of the British Crown, was to administer Sabah (which they named British North Borneo) until the end of the WWII.

The imposition of colonial rule did not go unchallenged, however. There were a number of rebellions, the most famous being led by a Bajau, Mat Salleh, who burned the settlement on Pulau Gaya off today's Kota Kinabalu in 1897, and who was eventually killed in 1900. Murut hilltribes living in Rundum, in Sabah's remote southwest, also rebelled against the British in 1915, but were brutally repressed.

Looking for workers to labour in the rubber estates and tobacco plantations which they established in Sabah, the British imported large numbers of Chinese and Javanese, many of whom remained to eventually become Sabahan. Despite the planting of crops such as coconuts, sugar, hemp, tobacco and rubber, British North Borneo never brought the vast riches that its colonial rulers had envisaged. Tropical hardwood was difficult to extract from the forest prior to the introduction of modern machinery in the 1960s, but it made an important contribution to the colonial coffers.

In the years up until WWII, the infrastructure of North Borneo was slowly developed, yet the challenging nature of the terrain meant that roads were very limited. Transport between the various settlements—from Tawau on the far southeast coast up to Sandakan, around the northern tip to Kudat and down the west coast to the settlement of Jesselton (as Kota Kinabalu was then known)—was by steamer, while inland trails were travelled either on foot, pony or even water buffalo.

The construction of a railway line from Jesselton south to Papar and Beaufort, and on through the Padas River gorge to Tenom, contributed greatly to the development of the agriculturally rich interior valley running from Tenom northwards to Ranau. From 1905

Sutera Harbour Resort

Sutera Harbour Resort

Above: Sabah has the only rail service in all of Borneo, linking the capital with Tenom in the interior. An old steam train has been renovated and offers a leisurely way for visitors to discover the countryside between Kota Kinabalu and the small town of Papar.

onwards, rubber, rice, fruits and other produce were sent by rail to Jesselton. This railway line—the only one in Borneo—is in use up until today, although it now carries considerably more passengers than freight.

The invasion of the Japanese during WWII began a harsh period for the people of North Borneo. Their previous colonial administrators were either shipped to prisoner-of-war camps in Kuching, or sent to work on the notorious Burma railroad. The local people suffered from food shortages and lack of medical care, while the Chinese were particularly brutally treated. Showing great courage and a strong commitment to the land that had become home, a group of local Chinese master-minded the region's only Chinese-led rebellion against the Japanese in 1944. The rebellion failed and its leader, Albert Kwok, and 175 others were executed by the Japanese.

Right: A group of Kadazandusun women and children photographed at Kampung Kiau, on the lower slopes of Mt Kinabalu, in 1939. The backpacks seen here are still used today for carrying fruit, vegetable and rice.

V.W. Ryves

Left: A view of Sandakan, capital of British North Borneo until the end of WWII, seen from Government House, October 1887.

The relief of North Borneo by Allied troops, led by the Australian armed forces, was preceded by heavy bombing to dislodge the Japanese. This resulted in the total destruction of Sandakan, the capital of British North Borneo since 1884, with not one building in the commercial area left standing. As slightly less damage had been inflicted upon the town of Jesselton, a decision was made to move the capital here from Sandakan. Lacking the resources needed to rebuild North Borneo after the end of the war, the North Borneo Company handed it to the British Crown. It became a colony, and the slow process of rebuilding began.

The move towards independence that swept Southeast Asia after WWII resulted in the colony of North Borneo gaining its independence in 1963, when it reverted to its original name of Sabah. Shortly afterwards, Sabah, along with neighbouring Sarawak, joined in the formation of the Federation of Malaysia on 16 September 1963. The colonial name of Jesselton (which commemorated Sir Charles Jessel, a director of the Chartered Company), was changed in 1967 to Kota Kinabalu, literally "The City of Kinabalu".

W.M. Poon

Chapter 3

The Mountains

The most dramatic feature of Sabah is the 4,095-metre mountain after which the capital city is named: Kinabalu. The tallest peak between the Himalayas and New Guinea, it dominates the landscape and legends of the Kadazandusun people, and is literally the high point of the 754-square-kilometre Kinabalu Park. The importance of Kinabalu's botanical diversity is such that the Park—which holds what one expert described as "one of the richest assemblages of plants in the world"—was declared a World Heritage Site (Malaysia's first) by UNESCO in November 2000. Apart from being the most striking physical feature of Sabah, Mount Kinabalu is a magnet for the adventurous, who come to scale the highest mountain in this part of Southeast Asia.

Almost twice the height of the surrounding mountain range, Mount Kinabalu appears to be even higher than it is. As one early visitor put it: "it rises sheer and wonderful above a thousand hills ... it is no wonder that natives hold it in veneration as the resting place of departed spirits and a dragon's home". The mountain exerts a magical quality that is difficult to define, changeless yet ever changing. At times, its brooding bulk seems almost malevolent, then as wisps of cloud catch on its granite peaks, the mountain plays like a beautiful woman peeping coyly from behind a veil. Suddenly, as the clouds are torn away by the wind, the summit reveals a mass of twisted pinnacles, like petrified flames leaping up into the sky.

Most of Sabah is mountainous, with swampy coastal areas fringing much of the east coast, and narrow fertile plains ending in sandy beaches along the

C.L. Chan

Opposite: The summit of Mt Kinabalu, frequently surrounded or covered by clouds, is a powerful magnet for climbers and nature lovers alike. **Above:** A small forest gecko peers out from its perch on a leaf; Kinabalu Park is rich in reptiles, some of them endemic.

21

Discovering Sabah

Opposite above: Three members of the prolific ginger family. Over 30 species of ginger are found in Kinabalu Park. **Opposite below:** After heavy rains, dozens of waterfalls course down the granite flanks of the mountain. **Below left:** Pitcher plants are found between 1,500 and 3,350 metres in Kinabalu Park; this beautiful specimen is a *Nepenthes rajah*. **Below right:** The dramatic crags known as the Donkey's Ears; there are more than 12 peaks over 3,600 metres on the summit plateau. **Following pages:** Mt Kinabalu, viewed from the west coast, dominates the landscape.

west coast. The main chain of mountains, the Crocker Range, runs roughly north to south and consists of very steep mountains averaging about 1,000 to 1,500 metres in height. The only pass through this formidable natural barrier between the interior and the west coast is the gorge carved by the Padas River. This rises in the mountains near the tiny village of Long Pasia and carries most of the rain falling on southwest Sabah via the gorge and the town of Beaufort out to sea at the southern side of the swampy Klias peninsula.

The Crocker Range National Park (almost 1,400 square kilometres in size) is Sabah's biggest park and was set aside largely to protect the water catchment area for the west coast. Although there are a few rudimentary trails and lookout points in this park, its attractions are eclipsed by the even more remarkable Kinabalu Park.

Climbing to the summit would be sufficient reason to justify a visit to Kinabalu Park. But the summit plateau—where more than a dozen peaks thrust up more than 3,600 metres from a solid core of granite—is only one of the many attractions within the Park.

Charles Clarke

Susan K. Jacobson

Susan K. Jacobson

Anthony Lamb

Anthony Lamb

Cede Prudente

Nexus Resort Karambunai

C.L. Chan

Anthony Lamb

Anthea Phillipps

Right: The summit trail leads relentlessly upwards, but climbers are rewarded by a changing array of plants, depending upon the altitude and soil. **Above top:** The Kinabalu Balsam grows by streams and waterfalls. **Above:** One-third of the 900 species of rhodendrons found in the world grow in Borneo, with 35 of them found in Sabah. Rhododendrons are often seen flowering along the trail on Mt Kinabalu, where around 25 species have been recorded.

Today's visitor generally approaches Mount Kinabalu from Park Headquarters on the southern side of the mountain, where accommodation, administrative buildings, restaurants and other facilities have been established at an altitude of 1,500 metres. However, the first non-Kadazandusun to climb to the summit plateau in 1851, Sir Hugh Low, had to head east from the Tuaran River, crossing the Tempasuk plain before trekking upwards through the thickly forested and rugged terrain on the southwestern side mountain, accompanied by his party of 42 porters and guides.

Low reached the summit plateau after a seven-day journey, but failed to find the highest peak. On his second trip in 1858, Low was accompanied by the adventurous Spenser St John, who succeeded in scaling South Peak (3,933 metres) while poor Low was prevented from making the ascent by badly injured feet. The honour of being the first foreigner to reach the true summit, in 1887, went to English zoologist John Whitehead, who named it Low's Peak.

C.L. Chan

Today's climber generally does the summit ascent and return in two days, leaving Park Headquarters and climbing along a well-maintained trail from the power station at 1,874 metres and spending the night at a rest house, hostel or huts at Laban Rata, at 3,280 metres. After an early start the next morning, climbers use ropes to guide them up the steep granite slopes and then trek across the summit plateau to Low's Peak.

Tengku D.Z. Adlin

Above: Many of the most striking flowers found in the mountains grow on the forest floor, their vivid colours contrasting with the dull leaf litter. This plant, actually a fungus, is unattractively known as the Red Rayed Stinkhorn and is found in Borneo's montane regions. **Left:** The summit of Mt Kinabalu, seems to have torn through a thick blanket of cloud.

27

Right: The almost sheer granite slopes leading to the summit contrast dramatically with the alpine vegetation found at around 3,000 metres, where trees are stunted and twisted by the winds. **Below:** Much of the alpine vegetation is similar to species found in New Guinea, New Zealand and parts of eastern Indonesia.

Chin Shui Hiung

Right: Squirrels living along the Kinabalu summit trail have learned that food is readily available from climbers who stop to rest in the shelters. Somewhat similar in appearance, the Mountain Treeshrew is found in Kinabalu Park and in the forests of the Crocker Range.

Chin Shui Hiung

Chin Shui Hiung

Right: The main trail to the summit starts at Timpohon Gate, reached by road from Kinabalu Park Headquarters. **Opposite left:** Plates of granite on the summit plateau have been broken by alternating heat and cold. **Opposite right:** The sheer walls of Victoria Peak. **Opposite below:** Tengku D.Z. Adlin (far right) and Kinabalu Park Warden, Eric Wong (second from left) with expedition members on the 1987 traverse of Bowen's Route, linking the West and East Plateau. **Below:** Mt Kinabalu at sunset.

Chin Shui Hiung

Chin Shui Hiung

Tham Yau Kong

Tengku D.Z. Adlin

Sualim Takun

Right: Mt Kinabalu, seen from the north. **Below:** A weary climber rests on the granite slabs flanking the western slopes of Mt Kinabalu. The white bands running through the rock are aplite dykes. **Opposite:** The side of South Peak is thought, by some, to show the face of a man with an eye, nose and mouth formed by grooves in the rock. **Following pages:** An aerial view of the jagged granite peaks of Mt Kinabalu's summit.

Anthea Phillipps

A yawning chasm to the east of the summit, Low's Gully, almost splits the mountain in two. This dramatic gully, plunging 3,000 metres in its seven-kilometre length, remained unconquered until an expedition in 1998—blessed by unusually dry weather—managed to abseil down vertical walls, edge along cliffs and swim over lagoons to emerge victorious.

John Briggs

The extreme diversity of plant life within Kinabalu Park is the result of differences in height, climate, soil and physical geography. A hike up the summit trail is the best way to view the changing plant life, with everything from buttercups to bamboos, insect-eating pitcher plants to the world's largest flower, the Rafflesia. There are eerily beautiful mossy forests where lichen and moss hang like mist caught in the branches, and sub-alpine forest where among the stunted trees, raspberries, leptospermum and some tenacious orchids are found.

Walks along the trails around Park Headquarters reveal a magnificent array of vegetation typical of the lower montane region, as well as views out over the forested hills, across to waterfalls and down over isolated villages clinging to the steep hillsides. Many of Mount Kinabalu's birds can easily be spotted from the roads around Park Headquarters, the most common being

Cede Prudente

Tengku D.Z. Adlin

Tham Yau Kong

Courtesy of the Royal Botanic Gardens, Kew

Anthony Lamb

Charles Clarke

Opposite, top: Climbers use a rope to guide themselves to the peak of Mt Kinabalu. This is named after the first foreigner to attempt to reach the summit, Hugh Low **(opposite, below left)**, then the British Resident based in Labuan.

Opposite, below right: Low's rhododendron is one of 24 species found around Mt Kinabalu. **Left:** Many plants on Mt Kinabalu are named after Hugh Low, who made two separate expeditions (1851 and 1858). This beautiful pitcher plant, *Nepenthes lowii*, was discovered by Low on his first ascent of the mountain, and is also found on many mountains in Sabah.

Below left: Both blackberries and raspberries grow above 1,200 m; this blackberry is named *Rubus lowii*. **Below:** Low's Buttercup (*Ranunculus lowii*) is found only on Mt Kinabalu, between 2,750–3,950 m, where it clings to damp pockets of soil.

C.L. Chan

C.L. Chan

Loi Pui King

the large beige-and-black Malaysian Treepie, the Ashy Drongo and the Chestnut-Capped Laughing Thrush. A walk at night with a good torch may reveal exquisite luminous fungi and stick insects up to 25 cm in length.

Some of Kinabalu Park's most interesting plants have been gathered together in the Mountain Garden, including pitcher plants, various species of rhododendron, and orchids, ranging from tiny flowers scarcely bigger than a grain of rice up to glorious and highly endangered slipper orchids. A self-guided trail which crosses into the forest from the Mountain Garden offers an excellent insight into the typical lower montane forest.

Park Headquarters is just one of four regions of Kinabalu Park accessible by vehicle. Some 40 kilometres away from Headquarters, Poring is popular primarily for its hot springs.

Mineral water which gushes out of the ground further up the mountain is channelled down into a series of individual baths, located both outdoors and inside bathing cabins. Thanks to its elevation of only 600 metres, Poring is a lushly beautiful region of giant *poring* bamboo (after which the region is named), fruit trees, hibiscus and spectacular gingers.

Previous pages: Mt Kinabalu, seen from the west, with the Tempasuk river in the foreground. Early expeditions to the mountain passed along this route, taking many days to reach Kg Kiau where the real climb began. **Above:** A beautiful adult male Black-hooded Oriole. **Right:** This conifer, endemic to Mt Kinabalu, is named after the first woman botanist to visit the mountain in 1913, Lilian Gibbs. **Opposite:** The eerily beautiful mossy forest of Mt Kinabalu, which grows between 1,200 and 1,800 m.

Anthony Lamb

40

Susan K. Jacobson

Mountain Orchids of Sabah

Jejewoodia jiewhoei.

C.L. Chan

Paphiopedilum rothschildianum.

C.L. Chan

Malaxis punctata.

C.L. Chan

Paraphalaenopsis labukensis.

C.L. Chan

Phalaenopsis amabilis.

Acanthephippium curtisii.

Trichoglottis jiewhoei.

Cleisocentron merrillianum.

Anthea Phillipps

Opposite & above: Despite the tremendous disparity in size, these huge Rafflesia blooms have something in common with delicate rosette sundews, as both are parasitic plants. The Rafflesia grows only on the Tetrastigma vine. **Left:** Looking like a terrestial equivalent of a sea anenome, these rosette sundews (a member of the Drosera family) have leaves covered with tiny hairs, making them a potential death trap for insects.

45

Anthea Phillipps

Wendy Hutton

Au Kam Wah

Wendy Hutton

Opposite: The giant *poring* bamboo, after which the hot springs area in Kinabalu Park is named. **Top:** The fun pools and water slides at Poring. **Above left:** The cool fresh water of the Rock Pool comes as a shock after the hot mineral water. **Above:** Rajah Brooke's Birdwing is one of the most striking butterflies at Poring. **Overleaf:** Mt Kinabalu is sacred to the Kadazandusun. A ritual sacrifice is carried out each year by a priest or *bobolian* at a small pool known as the Sacrifice Pool, located on the summit plateau.

W.M. Poon

Tengku D.Z. Adlin

Anthea Phillipps

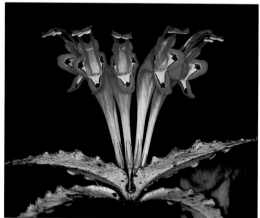

Above: The striking Lipstick Plant. **Right:** The seed cones of a conifer, *Agathis lenticula*, found only on the Crocker Range and on Mt Kinabalu.

Most of the bird and animal activity in the rain forest actually takes place in the canopy of the trees, high above the ground. Thanks to Poring's canopy walkway, anchored by three forest giants, visitors can literally have a bird's-eye view of the forest. Poring also has a large walk-in butterfly garden, where dramatically beautiful local butterflies can be seen. Among the most spectacular are the velvet black and iridescent green Rajah Brooke's Birdwing, and the equally lovely yellow and black Common Birdwing, while various insects such as huge stick insects and rhinoceros beetles can be seen in special netted areas.

With its hot baths, a Rock Pool with cold mountain water, a fun pool with a series of slides, picnic and camping areas, restaurants and accommodation, Poring Hot Springs is one of the most popular areas of Kinabalu Park. The more adventurous can follow a steep trail leading past a shallow cave where bats hang during the day on to an attractive waterfall, about 1 $^1/_2$ hours from the hot springs area of Poring.

Alternative accommodation to the Kinabalu Park Headquarters region is found at Masilau Plateau, on east side of the mountain beyond the 18-hole Kinabalu Golf Course. This recently developed area, located at 2,000 metres, gives an entirely new perspective of the mountain. An interesting trail running along a ridge offers stunning views of Kundasang far below, as well as glimpses up to the summit plateau. There is an easily accessible site where *Nepenthes rajah,* the largest of the pitcher plants found in Kinabalu Park, can be seen. The pitcher of this giant nepenthes can hold up to three litres of water, and Sir Hugh Low even reported finding a dead rat inside one pitcher.

On the west side of Kinabalu Park, accessible via Kota Belud and the picturesque village of Kampung Sayap, yet another ranger station and forest trails open up a less-visited side of the mountain. Although there is no accommodation at Kampung Sayap Station, there are several picnic areas, a camp site and an easily accessible and beautiful waterfall.

Opposite above: The summit of Mt Kinabalu is frequently covered by clouds, especially during the afternoon. On rare occasions during the southwest monsoon, from May until November, the crown of the mountain is encircled by a white cloud, while the lower slopes are completely clear. **Below:** A delicate begonia (*Begonia chlorocarpa*) found only on Mount Kinabalu. **Following pages:** The Kadazandusun living on the slopes of Mt Kinabalu and the Crocker Range are farmers, growing mainly rice, pineapples and other fruit. The traditional woven backpack is still the favoured way of transporting crops from the field.

C.L. Chan

51

W.M. Poon

Right: The Sacrifice Pool on the summit plateau, where the local Kadazandusun make an annual sacrifice to the spirits of the departed. During the Ice Age, the peaks on the summit plateau were thickly covered with ice.

Anthea Phillipps

Susan K. Jacobson

Left: Frogs are found in a variety of habitats, including on rocks along the streams, on the forest floor, on low-growing shrubs and up to the trees; this frog is the Kinabalu Tree Frog, found throughout the mountains of the Crocker Range.
Below: A land snail, with its translucent green shell the colour of a new leaf, feeding at night.

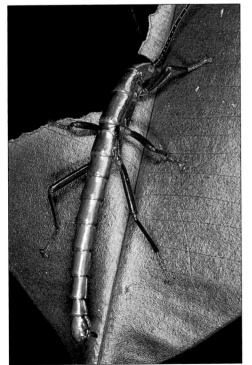

C.L. Chan

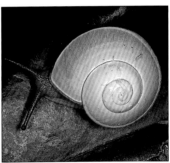

C.L. Chan

Above: A well-camouflaged spider awaits pollinating insects amongst the delicate flowers of a mountain orchid, *Eria robusta*.
Left: A stick insect, endemic to Mt Kinabalu. Most stick insects are cleverly camoflauged, and both patience and keen eyesight are required to spot them.

C.L. Chan

Tham Yau Kong

Above: The entrance to Kinabalu Park Headquarters. Located at 1,500 m, this region of the Park—which was declared a World Heritage Site in 2000, offers a range of accommodation and restaurants, souvenir shop, an interpretation centre and trails. **Right:** Accommodation at Park Headquarters offers everything from simple hostels with dormitories to twin-bed cabins and self-contained chalets, some with fire-places.

Au Kam Wah

Tommy Chang/STPC

Left: Chalets in native timber with ironwood shingles cling to the hillside at Masilau, on the east side of Kinabalu Park. The original vegetation has been left intact despite the construction of accommodation, a restaurant and information centre at an altitude of 2,000 m. A trail from Masilau links up with the main Kinabalu summit trail, which begins at Timpohon, near the Park Headquarters.

57

C.L. Chan

Above & right: A range of small hotels and larger resorts are located near Kinabalu Park; the Zen Garden is in a secluded valley not far from the vegetable markets of Kundasang.

C.L. Chan

Hotel Perkasa Mt. Kinabalu

Left: Perkasa Hotel sits on a hilltop in Kundasang, and has an unrivalled view of Mt Kinabalu.

Tommy Chang/STPC

Left: The highest golf course in Southeast Asia is located on the eastern slopes of Mt Kinabalu. The clubhouse is a fine place to relax and enjoy the view after 18 holes in the refreshing highland climate.

Right: The entrance to the Mountain Garden, located at Park Headquarters, where a wide range of plants (including orchids and pitcher plants) has been assembled. This acts as an introduction to some of the flora of Kinabalu Park. **Below:** This unusual orchid is aptly named the Boxing Glove Orchid.

C.L. Chan

W.M. Poon

60

W.M. Poon

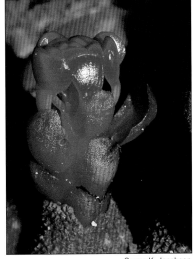

Susan K. Jacobson

Far left: The delicate yellowish-pink of one of the many fungi found in the mountainous regions of Sabah. Luminous fungi which glow in the dark can be seen at night in some montane and lower montane forest. **Left:** The flowers of a *Balanophora*, a leafless parastic plant that emerges from tubers that grow on the roots of a variety of host plants.

C.L. Chan

Left: Part of the Mountain Garden includes a short trail, where some of the plants have been labelled for easy identification. This trail crosses the Liwagu river.

61

Chapter 4

The Rain Forest

Entering a virgin rain forest is often an overwhelming experience, with life positively teeming on every level. Insects buzz and rasp and shrill, birds sing, frogs croak or boom, monkeys call, squirrels chatter, branches creak and you can almost hear young shoots of the plants as they grow rapidly towards the light.

Thanks to its tropical climate and lack of any marked dry season, Sabah's forests are among the most richly varied rain forests in the world. From the forest floor (where thousands of insects are busy in the decaying leaves, fallen branches and fungi), through the lower level of the forest (where lianas and palms and literally hundreds of other plants crowd each other in competition for the light), right up to the forest canopy where the trees can be more than 50 metres high, the rain forest is one of the most complex—and threatened—eco-systems in the world.

Cede Prudente

The tallest forest trees, members of the dipterocarp family, are commercially very valuable as hardwood timber. Much of Sabah's rain forest is being selectively logged to provide an important source of income to the state. Many other areas have been protected in forest reserves, parks and other conservation areas.

The flora and fauna of the rain forest depend largely upon altitude. The majority of Sabah's forest is lowland rain forest, including areas such as

Above: The beautiful Blue-winged Pitta is a migrant that can sometimes be seen in the lowland rain forest.
Opposite: The waters of this river in the Maliau Basin have a reddish tinge, owing to the tannin content from fallen leaves.

Danum Valley, Sepilok Forest Reserve, Tabin Wildlife Reserve and part of Kinabalu Park. From around 1,200 metres up to 2,000 metres, the forest is classified as lower montane and includes various oaks, conifers and myrtles; this type of forest is found on the Crocker Range (and includes the Rafflesia Forest Reserve), in Kinabalu Park and in the remote Maliau Basin.

One of the most accessible areas of rain forest, apart from Kinabalu Park, is the Sepilok Forest Reserve, 43 square kilometres of superb lowland rain forest located just 25 kilometres from Sandakan. Sepilok is famous for its Orang-utan Rehabilitation Centre, devoted to the conservation of one of the most remarkable creatures found in Sabah's rain forests.

The orang-utan—a gentle, shy ape found only in Borneo and Sumatra—is highly endangered, partly owing to the loss of its forest habitat. Animals which have been kept captive, or which have been disturbed by logging activities, are brought to Sepilok to have their health monitored and to be taught the necessary skills for returning to the wild. Visitors are permitted to watch the twice-daily feeding of the orang-utans, when the semi-wild apes

Above: One of the most elegant birds of the Bornean rain forest, the Greater Racket-tailed Drongo. **Right:** The best place to see the world's largest bloom is in the Rafflesia Forest Reserve in the Crocker Range, with more than 50 sites where this parasitic flower grows. This Rafflesia (*Rafflesia tengku-adlinii*) is named after Tengku D.Z. Adlin, one of Sabah's most noted conservationists.

Tengku D.Z. Adlin

Left: This escarpment forms part of the rim of the Maliau Basin, Sabah's "Lost World". **Below:** A Horned Toad, with projections which make it appear as if it is wearing a leaf as disguise.
Bottom: A Fireback Pheasant, one of Sabah's many striking birds. Danum Valley Conservation Area is one of the best locations for viewing Fireback, Argus and Bulwer's Pheasants.

C.L. Chan

Susan K. Jacobson

Wendy Hutton

Wendy Hutton

Tommy Chang/STPC

Opposite: The stunning seven-tier Maliau Falls, located in the Maliau Basin. **Below:** Cradled by a high limestone escarpment, the virginal Maliau Basin in the central southern region of Sabah is preserved for conservation and research. Many of Sabah's mammals, including the tiny mousedeer **(above left)** and perhaps the rare Asian Rhinoceros **(above)**, can be found here.

Tengku D.Z. Adlin

Cede Prudente

Previous pages: An aerial view of a lowland rain forest shows the density of the forest canopy. The diversity of the plant life is astonishing, with as many as 600–700 species of plant found in one hectare of rain forest, compared with as few as seven species in a typical temperate forest.

W.M. Poon

Above: A Buffy Fish Owl. **Right:** High rainfall, particularly in the montane rain forest, creates many waterfalls, cascades, rivers and pools ideal for bathing. This magnificent waterfall is one of the many found in the Danum Valley Conservation Area in Lahad Datu.

Sabah Air

Anthony Lamb

W.M. Poon

Francis Seow-Choen

Top: A dozen species of owl, a bird more often heard than seen, are found in Sabah, including the Scops Owl seen here. **Above:** The unmistakable "woop woop" of the Borneon Gibbon is a part of the morning chorus in the rain forest. **Left:** The Slow Loris, with its appealing large eyes and soft fur, is a relatively common primate in Sabah, where it is often found raiding cocoa plantations. Because it also feeds on insects which attack cocoa pods, it is seldom disturbed by plantation workers.

71

come to a wooden platform to enjoy milk and bananas. When the forest trees are fruiting, the number of orang-utans coming to feed diminishes, but at times when the pickings are lean, even some of the large males which have been successfully rehabilitated and are living wild in the forest return to the feeding platforms to enjoy a free meal.

Nearby the Sepilok Forest Reserve, the well-planned Rainforest Information Centre run by the Forestry Department has an excellent display on all aspects of the rain forest. Of particular interest is the section showing the traditional ways rainforest products have been used by Sabah's people: for food, medicine, household items, fuel and furniture. This is one of the best interpretation centres in Sabah, and well worth visiting; a short marked trail leading around a small lake next to the Rainforest Information Centre offers further insight on the rain forest.

Anyone with a serious interest in the rain forest and its plant and animal life will be rewarded by a visit to the Danum Valley Conservation Area, a 438-square-kilometre reserve set aside for research and education. The Borneo Rainforest Lodge, a series of wooden chalets set in virgin forest along a curve in the Danum River, offers a comfortable base for exploration. There

Above: An Osprey, one of the largest birds of prey found in Sabah. **Right:** Two species of Barking Deer or *munjak* are found in Sabah, as well as the larger Sambar Deer and Javan Rusa deer. Hunting has greatly reduced the numbers of deer, although they still thrive in protected areas of rain forest.

Tommy Chang/STPC

Wendy Hutton

C.L. Chan

Susan K. Jacobson

Above left: Before laws were passed to conserve Sabah's wildlife, hunters kept trophies of the animals they had captured for food. This man from Long Pa sia proudly shows off his necklace made from various teeth and claws. **Above right:** Unlike many insects in the forest, which resort to clever camouflage to avoid predators, this blue and black longhorn beetle flaunts its beauty. **Left:** Sulphur springs are found in Tawau Hills. This region of Sabah was once volcanic, a factor which contributes to the richness of the soil. Off the west coast, on Pulau Tiga, mud volcanoes are another sign of activity far below the earth's crust. **Following pages:** Sabah's rain forests offer many rare and beautiful plants.

W.M. Poon

Susan K. Jacobson

Wendy Hutton

Au Kam Wah

The rain forest produces a wide range of food, medicines and countless other useful products. These include honey from wild combs **(opposite)**, sour fruits **(left)** and *rotan* used to make all kinds of baskets and hats **(above)**.

C.L. Chan

C.L. Chan

Au Kam Wah

are a number of forest trails, including one leading past a small waterfall and pool ideal for swimming, on up to a ridge where ancient burial jars belonging to indigenous Orang Sungei have been found.

All of Sabah's mammals, including the elephant, orang-utan, bears and the extremely rare rhinoceros have been recorded at Danum, although the chance of seeing these in the rain forest is rare. Wild animals, especially the more endangered species, avoid human contact as far as possible. However, various species of monkeys can often be spotted, as well as flying squirrels, deer, civets and many other small mammals.

Danum's bird life includes all eight of the hornbills found in Sabah, as well as more than 230 other species ranging from the stunning Argus Pheasant to tiny vivid sunbirds. Bird-watching enthusiasts report that Danum is one of the prime areas in Sabah (the others being the Kinabatangan wetlands and Kinabalu Park).

A canopy walkway near the Borneo Rainforest Lodge offers a spectacular view of the forest in the valley below, and a chance to spot the nests built by orang-utans before they sleep at night. A night drive with spotlights will usually reveal some of the nocturnal creatures of the rain forest.

Opposite above: The Field Centre in the Danum Valley Conservation Area is a base for Malaysian and foreign scientists carrying out a wide range of research projects, as well as exploring methods of sustainable logging.
Opposite below: Located almost 50 kilometres from the Field Centre, the Borneo Rainforest Lodge offers visitors a comfortable base from which to explore the astonishing flora and fauna of Danum Valley's lowland tropical rain forest.

79

C.L. Chan

Above: The largest land tortoise in Asia can be found in the forests of eastern Sabah. **Right:** Mother and baby orang-utans. Because of their weight and lack of tails, orang-utan move slowly, relying on their strong arms. At night, they build a nest of branches in a tree top, and sleep safe from any disturbance on the forest floor.

Cede Prudente

Wendy Hutton

Cede Prudente

Top: A mature male orang-utan has come in from the forest for a free meal of bananas and milk at the Sepilok feeding platform, while a macaque waits hopefully for any left-overs. **Left:** Baby orang-utans.

C.L. Chan

C.L. Chan

Although the wildlife can be spectacular, the plant life of the rain forest, and the complex interaction between the plants and the various insects, birds and mammals, is just as fascinating. Both Danum Valley and Kinabalu Park offer huge areas of virgin rain forest with thousands of species of plants, while a smaller but particularly interesting region of lower montane forest can be explored in the Rafflesia Forest Reserve, on the Crocker Range, less than two hours' drive from Kota Kinabalu.

Above left: *Dendrobium cymboglossum*, a native orchid endemic to Sabah. Both native and hybrid orchids can be seen in the orchid centre at Sabah Agricultural Park, near Tenom.
Above right: A native lowland species, *Dendrobium anosmum*, has striking and sweetly scented blooms.

This forest reserve was set aside to protect the world's biggest flower, the Rafflesia. Borneo has seven species of this bizarre bloom. One of the most common local species averages 30 cm in diameter, althou gh the *Rafflesia keithii* can grow up to one metre across. The Rafflesia is actually a parasite that grows on the roots and stems of the *Tetrastigma* vine. It takes up to nine months for the bud to develop into a fleshy bloom, which emits a strong odour to attract flies and ensure pollination. The bloom lasts for only two or three days before fading and dying. There are more than twenty known locations where the Rafflesia grows in the Rafflesia Forest Reserve, with trails leading to several of them. In addition, there is an interesting information centre. The reserve spreads across steep hills covered with a rich and interesting vegetation, including orchids.

When the Maliau Basin—set in central southern Sabah and almost completely encircled by a high limestone escarpment—first came to public attention around a decade ago, it was referred to as Sabah's "Lost World". This remote and almost inaccessible region has never been inhabited by man, and exploration of its botanical riches was begun only recently. Thanks to differing soil composition, several types of vegetation exist and many plants found nowhere else in Sabah have been discovered. A long-term conservation and management programme is currently underway, and it may eventually be possible for visitors to explore the Maliau Basin.

W.M. Poon

While Maliau Basin is most interesting for its geological structure and plant life, Tabin Wildlife Reserve is, as the name indicates, primarily for the protection of Sabah's wildlife. This huge reserve located on the large peninsula on the northern side of Darvel Bay, northeast of Lahad Datu, was partially logged during the 1970s and 1980s, but the regrowth is sufficient to feed a population of elephants, wild cattle or *banteng* and even the rhinoceros. Currently, Tabin is devoted solely to conservation and research, although a certain amount of eco-tourism is expected to be permitted within the reserve.

Above: Although many types of snake (such as this Red-tailed Racer) are found in Sabah, most avoid humans and are seldom spotted. This species is known to some locals as *mansak punti* or "ripe banana".

Many plants growing wild in the rain forest are of vital importance to man, particularly for food and medicine. One place where such plants can be seen is the Sabah Agricultural Park, located near Tenom in a fertile valley less than four hours from Kota Kinabalu. The Agricultural Park offers a series of fascinating gardens, including several devoted to orchids and economic crops such as plants for beverages, spices, medicines and perfume. The Park has possibly the world's best Garden of Evolution (showing how plants evolved on earth), and apart from its many beautiful floral gardens, has a Honey Museum and a viewing platform for wild honey combs on a giant forest tree. The Park also offers recreation such as cycling, boating and camping.

Borneo is home to roughly 10 percent of the world's 25,000 species of orchid, and the largest collection of its native orchids is housed here at the Sabah Agricultural Park, which offers fascinating insights on how much man depends on the plants of the world's rain forests.

Chapter 5

Wetlands

With oozing mud, slithering amphibians, fish that "walk", birds that swim underwater and impenetrable thickets of mangrove, the coastal swamp is the least visited and perhaps the least appreciated environment in Sabah. Yet these swamps, which lie between the open sea and the dry land or freshwater swamps, are a vital part of the marine food chain. Here the decaying vegetation provides food for tiny organisms and crabs, which feed other creatures higher up the food chain such as fish, prawns and molluscs. Wetlands are important breeding grounds for birds, and coastal swamps protect the land from erosion, as well as acting as a filter between freshwater and the sea.

Indraneil Das

Although many of Sabah's mangrove swamps have been cleared for aquaculture or other development, large areas still remain, even within the boundaries of Kota Kinabalu. Twenty-four hectares of mangrove forest—all that remains of the extensive forest once found around Kota Kinabalu—have been preserved as part of the Likas Wetlands, just two kilometres from the city centre.

Part of the wetlands is occupied by the Kota Kinabalu City Bird Sanctuary, where boardwalks, bird hides and information panels helps visitors discover this fascinating environment. The nearby Likas Lagoon, easily visible from a coastal highway, provides another haven for many water birds, including species different to those found in the Bird Sanctuary. More

Above: An estuarine crocodile lurks on the banks of the Kinabatangan. Crocodiles are also found on the Klias peninsula on Sabah's west coast. **Opposite:** The Kota Kinabalu City Bird Sanctuary, with Mt Kinabalu in the distance, is located in the Likas Wetlands, only a few minutes from the centre of the city.

Susan K. Jacobson

Au Kam Wah

Opposite: At low tide, the roots of the mangrove trees are exposed. **Left:** The seed pods hang vertically from the trees; when sufficiently mature, they will drop directly into the soft mud where they will take root. **Below left:** The Rhinoceros hornbill, one of the most striking birds encountered in the wetlands and rain forests.

Cede Prudente

mangrove forest can be explored on Pulau Gaya, one of the islands forming the Tunku Abdul Rahman Marine Park off Kota Kinabalu; fiddler crabs, mud skippers (curious little fish which use their fins to move across the mud) and kingfishers are all readily spotted here. Further north, more mangrove forest has been protected along the Mengkabong River.

Another reasonably accessible area of mangrove swamp is around the huge bay of Sandakan, particularly the eastern reaches of the bay, where a maze of rivers meanders through the swamp forest to link up with the lower reaches of the Kinabatangan river. A trip by boat through these mangrove swamps—which form part of the largest wetlands area in all of Malaysia—and on up to the freshwater swamp forest of the Kinabatangan floodplain is a fascinating experience.

Above: A pair of Red Avadavat. **Right:** An immature proboscis monkey has reddish fur. **Opposite above:** The male proboscis monkey is perhaps the most striking inhabitant of the Kinabatangan wetlands. **Opposite below:** At dusk, groups of proboscis monkeys congregate along the river to socialise before sleeping.

The stunted mangrove trees, the only vegetation which will grow in brackish water, have roots that poke above the mud at low tide to allow them to obtain oxygen. Moving further away from the sea, the mangroves are gradually joined by *nipah* palms, which provide sugar from their inflorescences and are even more important for their thatch, traditionally used as roofing material. There are also spiky pandanus trees, members of the screwpine family whose leaves are woven to make baskets, mats and hats, and primitive cycads which look like palms but belong to a different botanical family.

Cede Prudente

This region is rich in birds, not just brilliantly coloured kingfishers with their raucous cries, but snakebirds or Oriental darters, which dive underwater to catch fish, herons and egrets. Both pig-tailed and long-tailed macaque monkeys are easily spotted where the freshwater swamp starts to take over from the salty mangrove forest, but the star of the Kinabatangan region is undoubtedly the proboscis monkey.

Found only in Borneo, the proboscis monkey is most remarkable, as the name suggests, for its nose. The mature male has an almost grotesque, pendulous fleshy nose, and as if that is not enough to live with, he also has a

Cede Prudente

Cede Prudente

89

huge pot belly. The female is roughly half the size of the male (which usually weighs over 20 kg), and has a dainty snub nose. Both monkeys have beautiful colouring, a mixture of orange and grey, with thick white tails.

Proboscis monkeys live in both mangrove and freshwater swamps, and have the habit of congregating in trees at the edge of the Kinabatangan and its tributaries in the late afternoon. They feed on the leaves of the *Sonneratia* tree and other plants, socialise, quarrel and make giant noisy leaps from tree to tree before finally sleeping. Proboscis monkeys have webbed feet and have been seen swimming in the rivers, although they need to be wary of the occasional crocodile.

Right: Herds of Asian elephants can sometimes be spotted in the Kinabatangan wetlands region. The east coast of Sabah is the only place in all of Borneo where elephants can be found. However, it is still uncertain whether these animals were introduced (perhaps as a gift from the Sultan of Sulu, who received them from the King of Siam) or are native to the region. **Below:** Eurasian Curlew.

Cede Prudente

C.L. Chan

C.L. Chan

Left above: Both Long-tailed and Pig-tailed macaques are easily spotted in the coastal and freshwater swamps. Unlike many other primates, they are surprisingly unafraid of humans.
Left below: A cicada emerges from its chrysalis. The loud, insistent shrill of the cicada is an unmistakable part of the rain forest chorus.

91

Right: Wild orang-utan can sometimes be spotted in the forests of the Kinabatangan floodplain. Both male and female adult orang-utan are solitary creatures. However, a mother will live together with her young for five to six years, teaching it to recognise edible plants, how to build a nest for sleeping and other essential skills.

Cede Prudente

Susan K. Jacobson

Right: An oxbow lake off the Kinabatangan river. The land around the Kinabatangan, from the mouth of the river until far inland, is known as a floodplain, as much of it is permanently waterlogged.

Cede Prudente

Visitors can stay in lodges along the Kinabatangan near the village of Sukau, and travel by small boat to watch the antics of this rare monkey in the late afternoon or in the early morning, when the mist rising from the river gives an ethereal feeling to the landscape. The proboscis monkey, engaging as it is, is far from being the only attraction along the Kinabatangan. Silver or red leaf monkeys, orang-utan and macaque can all be seen, while the area is also renowned for its small population of wild elephants (Sabah has the only elephants in Borneo). Crocodiles and otters live along the riverbanks, while a large number of strikingly beautiful birds (including several species of hornbill) are found here.

As Borneo's big rivers change course over the decades, old curves become isolated and eventually form what are known as oxbow lakes, which are generally rich in bird and animal life. An oxbow lake not far from Sukau can easily be explored by boat.

Above: A local fisherman checks the net he has strung across one of the streams in a mangrove area. The importance of mangrove swamps as vital breeding grounds for certain fish and other marine species is now recognised, and large areas have been conserved.

Tommy Chang/STPC

Tommy Chang/STPC

Above: The slender shape of egret standing on a partially submerged log is reflected in the still water. Egrets are a common bird in Sabah, found everywhere from the coastal swamps around Kota Kinabalu to paddy fields (where they are often seen together with water buffalo) to the rivers on the Kinabatangan floodplain.

Above: A Kinabatangan sunset. In the early morning, mist rising from the rivers and oxbow lakes gives this region a haunting beauty and makes the temperature surprisingly fresh. **Inset:** Freshwater prawns, a real delicacy, are often found along the Kinabatangan.

94

C.L. Chan

The Kinabatangan wetlands are such a vitally important environment that WWF, together with various government departments and non-governmental organisations, has embarked on a programme of research and conservation. This wetlands programme will assist in drawing up plans for the management of this priceless environment. Although some areas of freshwater swamp have been cleared and planted with oil palm, it is hoped that with proper management, the remaining wetlands will be preserved for the future.

Jason Isley/Scubazoo Images

Chapter 6

Beaches and Islands

The travel-poster dream of a tropical paradise with powder-white beaches, waving palms, and crystal-clear waters over colourful coral reefs is not a dream but the reality in Sabah. With almost 1,500 kilometres of coastline, Sabah has countless beautiful beaches. Although many of these are deserted, others offer luxurious resorts.

W.M. Poon

C.L. Chan

Opposite: Beauty above and below at Lankayan island. **Above:** A seed pod washed up on the shore. **Left:** Divers' chalets nestle on the edge of the beach on Pulau Sipadan, Sabah's most famous dive site regarded as one of the world's best.

Jones/Shimlock

Above: A snorkeler swims out over the edge of the reef on the north side of Sipadan, where the wall of coral drops 600 metres to the ocean floor.
Right: Pulau Sipadan, only 12 hectares in size, is Malaysia's only oceanic island, separate from the continental shelf of Borneo.

Michael Wong

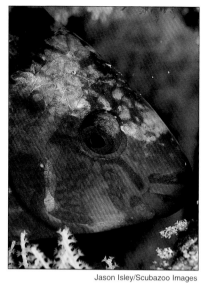

Jason Isley/Scubazoo Images

Jason Isley/Scubazoo Images

Top: A close-up of a Dusky Parrotfish. **Above:** One of the many colourful species of nudibranch, invertebrates found on coral reefs. **Right:** Turtles, strictly protected in Sabah, are unafraid of divers, enabling photographers to enjoy really close encounters.

Jason Isley/Scubazoo Images

Susan K. Jacobson

Islands dot the waters of the South China Sea, from Pulau Tiga (off the Klias Peninsula in southwest Sabah), far out to the Layang Layang Atoll and on up the west coast to the northern tip off Kudat. Even more islands lie in the Sulu Sea and the Celebes Sea off Sabah's northeast and eastern coast, including the Turtle Islands and Lankayan north of Sandakan, the Semporna islands and the Ligitan islands near the border with East Kalimantan.

Sea pearls, sea slugs or *bêche de mer,* dried fish and dried prawns were among riches that once attracted traders from the Sultanate of Sulu and as far away as China, and even today, fish are important for both local consumption and export. Sabah's waters are also home to giant sea turtles, manta rays, dolphins and a host of reef-dwelling fish, eels, molluscs and invertebrates. Sea birds—some of them rare migratory species—also nest on some islands. This richly varied marine environment is protected in several areas under the control of Sabah Parks, including Pulau Tiga, the five islands making up the Tunku Abdul Rahman Marine Park off Kota Kinabalu, the Turtle Islands Park north of Sandakan and the proposed Semporna Islands Park.

Above: Pulau Sapi is one of the most popular of the five islands in the Tunku Abdul Rahman Marine Park, just minutes from downtown Kota Kinabalu.

101

Jason Isley/Scubazoo Images

Above: Mabul, not far from Pulau Sipadan, offers interesting macro diving. **Right:** The luxurious Sipadan-Mabul Water Village perches directly on a coral reef.

Jason Isley/Scubazoo Images

Above: Divers returning to Pulau Mabul at dusk, after exploring the underwater world of the Celebes Sea.
Left: The huge fruits of a type of pandanus (*Pandanus dubius*). The more common *Pandanus odoratissimus*, known as the Seashore Screwpine, is usually found in the vegetation fringing Sabah's beaches.

103

Jason Isley/Scubazoo Images

Andrea e Antonella Ferrari

Above left & right: Corals come in an astonishing variety of shapes, sizes and colours, with soft corals looking more like plants than the rigid hard corals. **Right:** A school of huge Humphead Parrotfish, swimming off Pulau Sipadan.

Jason Isley/Scubazoo Images

Jones/Shimlock

Jones/Shimlock

Above: The beautiful but venomous Lionfish can usually be found swimming around wrecks off Pulau Lankayan, as well as on shallow reefs.
Left: An encounter with a manta ray can be an unforgettable experience.

105

Discovering Sabah

Opposite above: Pulau Selingan, the only island in the Turtle Islands Park where accommodation is available. **Opposite below:** Nesting turtles drag themselves laboriously on shore, where they dig a hole in the sand using their flippers; this turtle is returning to the sea after having laid her eggs.
Right: A turtle depositing her eggs. **Below:** A male turtle, recognisable by its long tail; male turtles very rarely go ashore.

Au Kam Wah

Tommy Chang/STPC

Cede Prudente

Au Kam Wah

Wendy Hutton

Above: Beaches line the west coast of Sabah, from the edge of the Klias Peninsula right up to the northwest tip of Borneo. Many of the beaches, like this one in Kudat district, are deserted except for the occasional fisherman or visitor enjoying a swim.

Opposite, above: Fishermen living off the east coast dry fish and seaweed, farmed in the waters of Darvel Bay, on platforms. **Opposite, below:** Lankayan Island Resort, north of Sandakan.

The teeming marine life of Sabah's undisturbed coral reefs, especially around the island of Sipadan, to the far southeast, is so outstanding that it attracts scuba divers from all over the world. Pulau Sipadan, Malaysia's only oceanic island, is like the head of a mushroom, sitting on a stem of coral almost 600 metres above the ocean floor. Divers become almost blase about swimming among sea turtles, schooling barracuda, white-tip sharks and other denizens of the deep, with a backdrop of multi-coloured hard and soft corals. As if all this marine life and beauty were not enough, Sipadan has undersea caverns which experienced divers can explore.

Sipadan and other islands nearby, including Mabul and Kapalai, offer accommodation and diving facilities, while islands north of Semporna, as well as Lankayan north of Sandakan offer scuba divers and island lovers a chance to indulge in their passion. The coral-fringed islands off Semporna are exceptionally beautiful.

In order to protect a group of islands where Green Turtles and Hawksbill Turtles come ashore to lay their eggs, the Turtle Islands Park was created in 1977. Limited accommodation on one of these islands, Selingan, makes it possible for visitors to stay overnight and see the turtles laying their eggs, and

Wendy Hutton

Jason Isley/Scubazoo Images

David Goh/Mantanani Resort

William Tan

Opposite: Pulau Manukan, the most developed island in the Tunku Abdul Rahman Marine Park, offers accommodation and other facilities. **Above:** A resort on the island of Mantanani, off Sabah's west coast. The island can be reached in about 45 minutes by speedboat from Usukun Bay, not far from Kota Belud. **Below:** Sunset from the beach at Mantanani.

Tee Kim Ling

Cede Prudente

to watch baby turtles racing for the sea after emerging from the egg about two months. The active conservation programme in force at the Turtle Islands helps ensure that these endangered marine creatures will continue returning to the beaches where they themselves were hatched, to lay their eggs and continue the cycle.

There are not many state capitals where forested islands fringed by white sandy beaches and coral reefs are only 15 minutes away by speedboat. Kota Kinabalu's residents and visitors alike are able to enjoy the beauty of the Tunku Abdul Rahman Marine Park, choosing an island to suit their taste. Pulau Gaya, the largest island closest to downtown Kota Kinabalu, is partly inhabited but the remainder is part of the park, with trails through the forest, a boardwalk through a patch of mangrove forest, several small beaches on the southern side and the glorious Police Beach on the north. Adjacent to the Park, at Gayana Resort, a private project to conserve the Giant Clam is being carried out.

Opposite: Pulau Berhala, off the town of Sandakan, has vertical sandstone cliffs on its southern side. It was once a leper colony, and during the early years of the Japanese Occupation, was a POW camp. **Below:** In an effort to provide an income for islanders around Semporna, seaweed farming is being encouraged. Here, harvested seaweed is brought ashore for drying; it is later processed and exported for use in the manufacturing of some food products.

Wendy Hutton

113

Just off the southwest tip of Gaya, the tiny island of Sapi is particularly popular for picnics and swimming with visiting tour groups. Pulau Manukan, the most developed island, has chalets for rental, a simple restaurant and a swimming pool, as well as small beaches. Mamutik, which is the training base for a leading dive operator, is a favourite with local visitors. Huge aru trees provide plenty of shade for the picnic tables, and from the two small beaches, there are dramatic views of the mainland, with the Crocker Range and even Mount Kinabalu often visible. The most remote island, Pulau Sulug, now offers facilities for scuba divers; part of the reef off the southwestern tip offers some of the best diving around Kota Kinabalu.

Below: The annual Lepa-Lepa festival is a time for boats around Semporna to take part in a range of competitions.

Damage done to the reefs of the Tunku Abdul Rahman Park (both by man and by a severe tropical storm in December 1996) has limited the range of corals and fish. However, patches of coral are slowly regenerating and given careful management, the diving and snorkeling potential of this beautiful region will eventually be realised.

Au Kam Wah

W.M. Poon

Tommy Chang/STPC

Wendy Hutton

Above right: The edge of the coral reef is clearly seen through the transparent waters off Semporna. **Above left:** Bajau, Suluk and Tausug fisherfolk prefer to live in stilt houses built over the reefs off Sabah's east coast. **Left:** A dive resort on Pandanan island, northeast of Semporna. Neighbouring Mataking island is home to another dive resort. There are plans for creating a Semporna Islands Marine Park nearby, around the islands of Bohey Dulang and Bodgaya.

115

Wendy Hutton

Above: A Bajau fisherman in front of the stilt village of Penambawan, in the Sulaman River north of Tuaran. Reached only by boat, this riverine *kampung* offers a glimpse of a way of life seems sure to disappear.

Pulau Tiga is accessible from the seaside town of Kuala Penyu (about one-and-a-half hours' drive from Kota Kinabalu), or by special boat charter directly from the capital city itself. Seldom visited even though Sabah Parks offers camping sites and a chalet, all this changed when a resort was developed on the southwestern side of the island, and Pulau Tiga was chosen as the location for the highly successful American TV series, *Survivor*.

Pulau Tiga now offers accommodation in chalets nestling under huge trees at the edge of the beach, with scuba diving and other non-motorised water activities available. Sabah Parks maintains a number of trails through the forest, one of them leading to the intriguing mud "volcanoes", where

116

Left: Located on the borders of the Tunku Abdul Rahman Marine Park on Pulau Gaya, this resort is not far from the city of Kota Kinabalu.

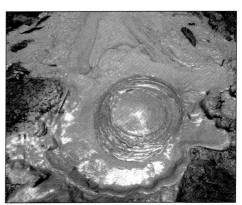

Wendy Hutton

Sipadan Dive Centre

Above: One of the mud volcanoes at Pulau Tiga Park, where the popular American TV series, *Survivor*, was filmed.
Left: Comfortable chalets in the Pulau Tiga Resort are a far cry from the "accommodation" experienced by the participants of *Survivor*.

Sipadan Dive Centre

117

Tommy Chang/STPC

Wendy Hutton

mineral-rich mud and gas slowly bubble up from deep underground. The island is also known for its shy megapodes, chicken-sized birds which lay their eggs in the sand and leave the sun to incubate them.

One hour plane by from Kota Kinabalu, Sabah's most remote dive location, Layang Layang, offers high adrenalin diving with almost endless visibility. An airstrip and luxurious accommodation have been built on the rim of the coral atoll, which drops off an astounding 2,000 metres to the ocean floor. Huge pelagic fish, hammerhead and other sharks, schooling jacks and other dramatic marine species can be seen here. A world-class diving location, Layang Layang is also an important nesting site for thousands of migratory sea birds.

Opposite: Visitors to the Rasa Ria Resort at Pantai Dalit, about 30 minutes north of Kota Kinabalu, have the choice of swimming in the sea or enjoying the huge free-form pool. **Above:** The wide range of recreational activities offered by the beautiful Nexus Resort, Karambunai, includes outdoor chess.

119

Jason Isley/Scubazoo Images

Simon Enderby/Scubazoo Images

Opposite: Layang Layang's airstrip and accommodation are built on the rim of a coral atoll far to the west of Kota Kinabalu. Its isolation ensures perfect underwater visibility. **Left & above:** Layang Layang is an important nesting site for thousands of sea birds, which lay their eggs directly on the ground.

An aerial view of the islands of the
proposed Semporna Islands Park,
north of Semporna. The hills of
Bodgaya and Bohey Dulang islands
are all that remains of the rim of an
ancient volcano.

Michael Wong

Tommy Chang/STPC

Chapter 7

Caves

Although Sabah's limestone caves might not be the most dramatic in Asia, their presence was largely instrumental in putting north Borneo on the map for Chinese traders many centuries ago. Some of these caves are home to two varieties of swiftlet which make the edible birds' nests highly prized by the Chinese for their medicinal qualities. Birds' nests were one of Borneo's most important trading items, and even today, nests harvested in Sabah's two main cave complexes are worth a fortune.

The riches produced by the swiftlets nesting in the Gomantong caves—once accessible via a tributary off the Kinabatangan river southeast of Sandakan—attracted the interest of the British North Borneo Company during the colonial era. They managed (after considerable resistance) to wrest control of the caves from traditional local harvesters. Today, the Gomantong caves are protected within a forest reserve, and harvesting of the nests is strictly controlled by the Wildlife Department to ensure the survival of the swiftlet population (or, to put it another way, to avoid killing the birds that make the golden nests).

A sealed road leading through the Gomantong Forest Reserve, a Visitor Centre and boardwalks leading right up to and around the inside of the main cave, Simud Hitam, make it easy for visitors to explore the area. During most of the year, activity within the caves is largely confined to the two million or so bats which fly out to forage for insects each evening. During the day, they

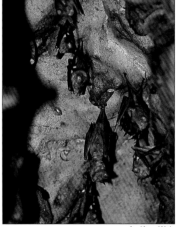

Au Kam Wah

Opposite: Harvesters prepare the rattan and bamboo ladder they use to reach the roof of the Gomantong Caves. **Above:** Colonies of bats, nocturnal feeders, can be found in all of Sabah's limestone caves. **Overleaf:** Madai Caves, with the small village in the foreground.

127

W.M. Poon

Wendy Hutton

Opposite: Visitors are dwarfed at the entrance of the Simud Hitam cave, part of the Gomatong cave complex. **Left:** In Madai caves, where this harvester is starting the dangerous climb to the roof, some of the caves walls have been painted or incised with decorations by workers.

C.L. Chan

C.L. Chan

Above: Specialised forms of life can be found in the gloom of the caves, including crabs and cockroaches. **Left:** The Cave Racer snake can be encountered in the guano on the caves floor

Au Kam Wah

129

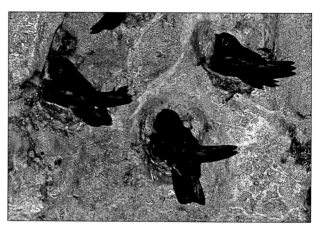

Right: Swiflets incubating their eggs. The gathering of their nests is controlled to ensure conservation.
Below: Nests grouped closely together on the walls of a cave. Experienced bird's nest dealers can tell from looking at a nest which region it came from.

Lim Chan Koon

Sabah Wildlife Department

Tommy Chang/STPC

Wendy Hutton

Wendy Hutton

Top: The cleaning of the nests is a painstaking task which must be done by hand. **Above:** Cleaned and dried nests packaged for sale. **Left:** The cave complex at Batu Punggul has still be to thoroughly explored. These caves are home to the Mossy Swiflet, whose nests are not edible.

131

S.P. Lim

S.P. Lim

drop waste products which form a layer of guano on the cave floor, a paradise for all kinds of beetles, cave cockroaches, centipedes and spiders. Outside the cave entrances, snakes and birds of prey wait their chance to pounce on the bats or injured swiftlets.

The main chamber of the Simud Hitam cave is split into two passage-ways, with light from holes in the cave roof streaming in and highlighting dangling rattan ladders and ropes.

During the harvesting season, this cave—and the slightly less accessible Simud Putih cave complex—comes alive with dozens of men risking their lives to gather the nests from the nooks and crannies of the cave walls and roof. Ropes which have been secured on the hill above the cave dangle through holes in the roof, and are lowered so that they can be used to pull up rattan ladders. An intricate system of ladders and notched bamboo poles, which look alarmingly precarious, helps the collectors climb as high as 90 metres to prise off the nests and transfer them into their rattan backpacks.

The swiftlets build their nests from edible saliva, generally between February and April. Immediately the nests have been made, they are gathered and the birds make a second nest. This is left undisturbed until the eggs have been laid and hatched, and the baby swiftlets literally flown the nest. This second batch of nests is gathered, some time between July and September.

The Gomantong caves are most spectacular during the harvest, yet any time of year, they are worth visiting. The forest reserve around the caves offers the opportunity of catching sight of some of Sabah's most beautiful birds, including the Scarlet Trogon, Asian Fairy Bluebird and Rhinoceros Hornbill.

The Madai cave complex, just off the main east coast road not far from the small town of Kunak, is perhaps even more fascinating than the Gomantong caves. The indigenous Ida'an, who converted to Islam more than four centuries ago, have owned rights to patches of these caves for as long as twenty generations. These rights are fiercely guarded, with the Wildlife Department assisting in the management of the caves, advising when nests should be harvested and collecting royalites for the government.

Anthony Lamb

A cluster of wooden shacks crowded near the entrance to the caves is virtually deserted during most of the year, with only a skeleton crew guarding each patch of cave against theft of the birds' nests. During the harvesting periods, this village comes alive with every house overflowing with workers, small shops doing a roaring trade, itinerant sellers of fabric and cigarettes, and women operating stalls selling cooked food and drinks for the collectors. The outer chambers of the Madai caves have several chalk drawings and paintings, while the inky depths of the interior are dominated by the collectors and all their paraphernalia.

Above: Two bright white eggs seem precariously balanced in this Mossy Nest Swiflet nest. Although the nests themselves are not made of edible saliva, the portion which fastens the nests to the walls is edible, and this is sometimes gathered and processed.

Other cave complexes in Sabah have revealed ancient remains, for it has long been the custom of some indigenous Borneo societies to bury their dead inside caves. Sometimes wooden coffins were used, although secondary burial, where the bones were placed inside ceramic jars traded by the Chinese, was also practiced. To protect these caves for future archaeological studies, they are not accessible to casual visitors.

Wendy Hutton

Chapter 8

From the Kampung to the City

Home is where the heart is, and for the people of Sabah, "home" is their *kampung* or native village. A Sabahan's *kampung* could be a thatched longhouse, a split-bamboo hut clinging to a mountainside, a comfortable wooden house on stilts surrounded by irrigated rice fields or a fishing village poised over the edge of a river or on a reef. It could also be a shophouse in a town, a modern brick terrace house or a suburban bungalow.

Because Sabah's people come from so many different ethnic groups, lifestyles vary considerably. Modernisation has meant that Sabahans from all ethnic groups can be found living in the towns and pursuing modern occupations, yet traditional lifestyles are still followed by a large percentage of the population.

Nearly all of Sabah's indigenous people once lived along the coast, in villages tucked into estuaries and rivers protected from the open sea. With the arrival of seafaring peoples from neighbouring countries, most of the original groups moved inland. Communities of Bajau, Irranun, Suluk,

Opposite: A Rungus longhouse in the Kudat district. **Left:** A Rungus girl in traditional dress. The Rungus are noted for their fine beadwork, weaving and basketware.

C.L. Chan

135

C.L. Chan

Cede Prudente

C.L. Chan

Wendy Hutton

Wendy Hutton

Obian, Tausug and other groups who began arriving during the 19th century (and continue to do so, despite efforts to stem the flow of illegal migrants) now dominate the coastal fishing villages and islands, particularly on Sabah's east coast.

Among the original indigenous coastal dwellers today are the Ida'an and Orang Sungei (who live mostly on Sabah's east coast) and the Bisayan and Brunei people living in the southwest, particularly around the Klias peninsula. The large and undeveloped island of Banggi, north of Kudat, is inhabited by the Banggi, a very small indigenous group whose language is totally unrelated to any of the four major linguistic groups in Sabah.

The biggest indigenous group, the Kadazandusun, live mostly in the interior regions of the state, particularly around Ranau and down the fertile plains stretching as far south as Tenom. They are also found along the west coast, from Kudat down to Beaufort. Many Kadazandusun are agriculturalists, growing non-irrigated or hill rice on the slopes of the Crocker Range, or irrigated rice on the coastal plains.

Above: Festive occasions in the villages or *kampung* always mean lots of food. This man from the Pitas district watches a huge pot of rice cooking over an open fire.

Opposite: Sabahans in traditional finery make an impressive sight. These include a Rungus couple **(above left)**, young Suluks **(above right)** and a Kadazandusun priest or *bobolian* **(below left)**. The young boy **(below right)** in a traditional baby carrier is too tired to enjoy the fun.
Following pages: Water buffalo are highly prized by local farmers.

137

W.M. Poon

Wendy Hutton

The Rungus, a sub-group of the Kadazandusun, are Sabah's most traditional ethnic group and live in the Kudat district on the northwest coast. Many Rungus still live in longhouses, communal dwellings where each family has their own sleeping and cooking quarters but shares a long verandah. Rungus longhouses have a unique architecture, very different from the better known longhouses of Sarawak, and unlike those of the neighbouring state, are built quite low to the ground and far away from rivers.

A community of Rungus living at Kampung Bavanggazao have built a couple of traditional thatch longhouses with sufficient modern comforts (such as separate bathroom facilities) to make them appealing to foreign visitors. A

Above: A Rungus woman at Kampung Bavanggazo, near Kudat. **Above left:** Local markets are often full of cultural colour. **Opposite above:** The west coast Bajau are renowned for their horsemanship; on festive occasions, both they and their horses are gaily decorated. **Opposite below:** A Dusun Tindal wedding couple.

141

Right: Gongs—and their players—come in all sizes. This Rungus baby could not resist trying his hand at the gong his father had just been playing.
Below right: Murut musicians dressed in the beaten bark cloth for which the Murut are noted. The Murut, a group of several different tribes, live in southwest Sabah, and were renowned hunters. **Below:** A young Rungus girl in traditional costume.

Wendy Hutton

Yong Lee Ming

Wendy Hutton

Tommy Chang/STPC

Above: The crossed poles at the apex of the roof are a typical feature of Bajau houses. These houses in Kampung Penambawan on the west coast also have walls of thatch, known locally as *attap*. **Left:** Large clusters of wooden houses with thatched roofs are built on the shallow reefs around Semporna on the east coast of Sabah. Most of the east coast Bajau prefer to live over the sea, where they seek their livelihood as fishermen.

143

Right & below: Many older women in Sabah are skilled weavers, making baskets and weaving fabrics on a back-strap loom.

Wendy Hutton

W.M. Poon

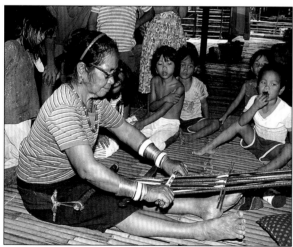

Wendy Hutton

Right: The traditional hearth of a kitchen in the remote village of Long Pasia. Damar, a form of resin gathered in the forest, is still used by the Lundayeh people to start fires.

Wendy Hutton

Cede Prudente

Above: Brightly coloured food covers are a standard item
on sale at the Sunday market or *tamu* held at Kota Belud.

145

Wendy Hutton

Susan K. Jacobson

Opposite: Newly harvested rice grains being spread out to dry in Tambunan. **Left:** Harvesting the rice with a special hand-held knife is a demanding business. It's no wonder that the end of a successful harvest is a time for celebration. The annual Pesta Ka'amatan or Rice Festival is Sabah's most important for the indigenous Kadazandusun.

Wendy Hutton

Left: A Rungus woman, wearing the customary wide armbands of a married woman, cleans and sorts tiny freshwater fish caught in a nearby stream. Although many Rungus live not far from the coast, they are farmers rather than fishermen, and often trade their vegetables for fish with the coastal Irranun and Obian people.

147

Right: An Indian provision stall in Kota Kinabalu market. Although a small community of Sikhs came to Sabah in the late 19th century, other ethnic Indians came in search of economic opportunities only after the formation of Malaysia. **Below:** A lively corner of the main market at Sandakan. Sabah's larger markets not only sell fresh food and dried provisions, but also offer kitchen equipment, clothing and shoes. In Sandakan market, it is even possible to find leech socks for protection in the rain forest.

Wendy Hutton

Cede Prudente

night at such a long house offers the rare opportunity to experience the customs, music, dance and cuisine of this group of traditional Sabahans.

The Murut, a group of several different, yet related, tribes living in the hilly areas around Tenom and in the southwest portion of the state, once lived in longhouses like the Rungus. Although a few scattered longhouses still remain along rivers such as the Sapulut, most Murut now live in single-family dwellings and make a living from small-scale agriculture.

Below: Bajau women carrying trays of prepared food, covered with the traditional woven food covers, as they walk along one of the jetties in a west coast stilt village.

W.M. Poon

Right: Lundayeh men performing a dance showing how a hunter stalks his prey. The man on the right is wearing fur, claws and teeth of animals he has captured while hunting. Some Lundayeh people still live in very remote communities, relying largely on the forest and rivers for food.

Tommy Chang

Wendy Hutton

Above: A Lundayeh woman wearing valuable antique beads strung in necklaces and made into a cap. **Opposite above:** The magnificent Kota Kinabalu City Mosque. **Opposite below:** 'Fook Teck Temple', Kudat.

In the far southwestern tip of Sabah, near the border of Sarawak, a small Lundayeh community lives in the remote village of Long Pa Sia. This hilly region at the source of the Padas river was once covered in virgin rain forest and offers a glimpse of an ethnic group which spreads across borders into both eastern Kalimantan and Sarawak. During the period known as *Konfrontasi*, when Indonesia's President Sukarno challenged the formation of Malaysia and attacked both Sabah and Sarawak, an airstrip was built at Long Pa Sia and British forces stationed here to guard against attacks from the Indonesian side of the border.

The Bajau—now the second biggest group of indigenous Sabahans after the Kadazandusun—have two different communities, each with their own language. Those living on the east coast, particularly around Semporna, concentrate on fishing, while the Bajau of the Kota Belud district on the west coast have become agriculturalists and raise cattle and ponies. They are well known for their skills as horsemen, almost all the jockeys at the local races being Bajau. On festive occasions, Bajau men dress both themselves and their horses, making a spectacular display.

W.M. Poon

W.M. Poon

C.L. Chan

C.L. Chan

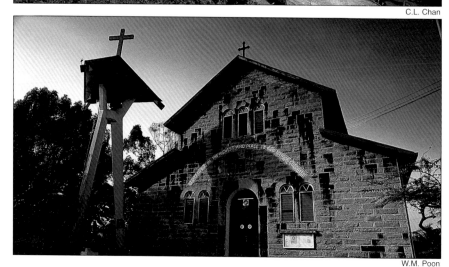

W.M. Poon

Opposite: The three buildings of the Sabah Museum in Kota Kinabalu, with their distinctive architecture. **Above top:** The Sabah State Mosque. **Above centre:** The Pu Jih Shih Buddhist Temple in Sandakan has a stunning view over the bay. **Above**: St

152

W.M. Poon

Right: The Kota Kinabalu International Airport is the second busiest in Malaysia. It has direct connections to a number of foreign countries, as well as local flights and connections with Sarawak and Peninsular Malaysia.
Below: Berringis Resort. Attractively priced resorts can be found along the coast between Kota Kinabalu and the southern town of Papar.

C.L. Chan

Tommy Chang

Nexus Resort Karambunai

Nexus Resort Karambunai

Above and following pages: Nexus Resort is located in the huge Karambunai complex north of Kota Kinabalu, offering golf as well as a wide range of other recreational activities. **Left:** The Nexus Resort organises an annual sea carnival, where dragon boat races are part of the fun.

155

Tee Kim Ling

Tee Kim Ling

Discovering Sabah

Previous pages & right: Sabah has many luxurious resorts in or near Kota Kinabalu, as well as in several other locations. Sutera Harbour Resort—the glorious paradise framed by serene tropical islands in the South China Sea, with majestic Mount Kinabalu as its backdrop—is only five minutes from the city centre of Kota Kinabalu and 10 minutes from the international airport.

Sutera Harbour Resort

Right: The Shan-Shui golf course north of Tawau is regarded by many as Asia's best.
Opposite above: The Borneo Golf & Country Club at Bongawan (an hour's drive south of Kota Kinabalu), was designed by Jack Nicklaus.

Shan-Shui Golf & Country Club

Bongawan Golf & Country Club

The Chinese, who were first brought in large numbers to British North Borneo during the 1880s, are a very visible part of the population, particularly in the towns where they dominate commerce and trading. Like the Chinese in neighbouring Sarawak, a large number are Christian and there has been a considerable amount of intermarriage with indigenous Sabahans, particularly with Kadazandusuns.

The timber industry, dominated by the Chinese, provided an enormous amount of wealth for the state during its heyday in the 1960s and 1970s. At that time, Sandakan was reported to contain more millionaires than any other town its size in the world. In recent years, however, the state economy is increasingly dominated by another form of green gold: palm oil. Thousands of hectares of oil palms cover the state, especially along the east coast where the terrain is less abrupt, having replaced rain forests. Many of these estates, including the huge Sahabat estate (reported to be one of the largest oil palm estates in the world), are owned by public listed companies.

Following pages:
Shangri-La's Tanjung Aru Resort was Sabah's first, and enjoys a superb location with close proximity to Tanjung Aru beach, the islands of the Tunku Abdul Rahman Marine Park and the city.

161

Tee Kim Ling

C.L. Chan

Above: Weekly markets, known as *tamu*, are colourful affairs when people come from far and wide to buy and sell. Kota Belud, less than an hour north of Kota Kinabalu, is renowned for its *tamu*, held every Sunday.

Rubber was the most important crop during the colonial era, and thousands of Javanese labourers were brought in to labour in estates along the west coast and in the Interior, especially around Tenom. Many Javanese remained and made Sabah their home, with Christians from Timor and Flores arriving to swell the numbers originally from Indonesia. It is the Bugis, from Sulawesi, who are the dominant Indonesian group today, most of them working as labourers in the oil palm estates, or on fishing boats in Sabah's coastal waters.

Since the formation of Malaysia, Indians and Malays from Peninsular Malaysia have come seeking business opportunities in Sabah. A small group of Sikhs, brought to British North Borneo as policemen and soldiers during the early colonial period, remained to become Sabahan. Most of them live around Kota Kinabalu.

During the late 19th and early 20th centuries, with so many different ethnic groups—some of them with a history of engaging in head-hunting—opportunities for tension were bound to exist. To provide a neutral meeting ground, the British North Borneo Company introduced the *tamu*, a market where people could meet to buy, sell and, even more important, socialise. Even today, in the era of supermarkets, the *tamu* remains an important part of life in Sabah. The weekly *tamu* are frequented by locals who bring their own home-grown or home-made produce, as well as traders from the towns, who come with their vans filled with shiny plastic, cheap clothing, kitchen utensils, knives, tools and shoes.

A visit to a *tamu* is a perfect opportunity to see farmers and fishermen mingling, to watch water buffalo being traded, to buy honey or hill rice or handicrafts. Some of the most famous *tamu* close to Kota Kinabalu include the Sunday markets at Tuaran and Kota Belud, the Wednesday market at Tamparuli and the Thursday market at Nabalu, not far from Kinabalu Park.

Even Kota Kinabalu has its version of a *tamu*, the Gaya Street Fair held every Sunday morning. Jalan Gaya is transformed into a thriving market where stalls sell everything from pet rabbits to fruit tree seedlings, dried medicinal herbs to live aquarium fish, home-made cakes to second-hand bric-a-brac.

Even in the city, Sabahans are never far from the *kampung*.

Tommy Chang/STPC

Left: Sabah's succulent seafood is a great favourite with visitors.

Further Reading

Mount Kinabalu: Borneo's Magic Mountain—an introduction to the natural history of one of the world's great natural monuments *by* K.M. Wong & C.L. Chan

Enchanted Gardens of Kinabalu: A Borneo Diary *by* Susan M. Phillipps

A Colour Guide to Kinabalu Park *by* Susan K. Jacobson

Kinabalu: The Haunted Mountain of Borneo *by* C.M. Enriquez (Reprint)

Visitor's Guide—Kinabalu Park—Sabah, Malaysian Borneo *by* A. Phillipps & Francis Liew

A Walk through the Lowland Rainforest of Sabah *by* Elaine J.F. Campbell

The Larger Fungi of Borneo *by* David N. Pegler

Pitcher-plants of Borneo *by* Anthea Phillipps & Anthony Lamb

Nepenthes of Borneo *by* Charles Clarke

Slipper Orchids of Borneo *by* Phillip Cribb

Birds of Mount Kinabalu, Borneo *by* Geoffrey W.H. Davison

The Birds of Borneo (Fourth edition) *by* Bertram E. Smythies (Revised by Geoffrey W.H. Davison)

Proboscis Monkeys of Borneo *by* Elizabeth L. Bennett & Francis Gombek

The Natural History of Orang-utan *by* Elizabeth L. Bennett

A Field Guide to the Frogs of Borneo *by* Robert F. Inger & Robert B. Stuebing

A Field Guide to the Snakes of Borneo *by* Robert B. Stuebing & Robert F. Inger

The Natural History of Amphibians and Reptiles in Sabah *by* Robert F. Inger & Tan Fui Lian

Layang Layang: A Drop in the Ocean *by* Nicolas Pilcher, Steve Oakley & Ghazally Ismail

The Dragon of Kinabalu and other Borneo Stories *by* Owen Rutter (Reprint)

Land Below the Wind *by* Agnes N. Keith (Reprint)

Three Came Home *by* Agnes N. Keith (Reprint)

White Man Returns *by* Agnes N. Keith (Reprint)

Forest Life and Adventures in the Malay Archipelago
    by Eric Mjöberg (Reprint)

A Naturalist in Borneo *by* Robert W.C. Shelford (Reprint)

Twenty Years in Borneo *by* Charles Bruce (Reprint)

An Introduction to the Traditional Costumes of Sabah
    (eds. Rita Lasimbang & Stella Moo-Tan)

A Field Guide to the Mammals of Borneo
    by Junaidi Payne & Charles M. Francis

Pocket Guide to the Birds of Borneo *Compiled by* Charles M. Francis

Kinabalu: Summit of Borneo (eds. K.M. Wong & A. Phillipps)

Traditional Stone and Wood Monuments of Sabah *by* Peter Phelan

Rafflesia: Magnificent Flower of Sabah *by* Kamarudin Mat Salleh

Borneo: the Stealer of Hearts *by* Oscar Cooke (1991 Reprint)

Traditional Cuisines of Sabah (ed. Rita Lasimbang)

Cultures, Costumes and Traditions of Sabah, Malaysia: An Introduction

Tamparuli Tamu: A Sabah Market *by* Tina Rimmer

Sabah, Malaysian Borneo: People & Places
    by Tommy Chang and Wendy Hutton

Insight Pocket Guides: Sabah, Borneo *by* Wendy Hutton

Sabah & Sarawak with Brunei Darussalam (ed. Wendy Hutton)

PUBLISHER'S ACKNOWLEDGEMENTS

The Publisher would like to thank the following individuals and organisations for their valued contribution to this book:

Y.A.B. Datuk Chong Kah Kiat, Chief Minister and Minister of Tourism, Environment, Science and Technology, Sabah, for his interest in the project and valued comments. Datuk Monica Chia, Permanent Secretary, Ministry of Tourism, Environment, Science and Technology, Sabah, for her unfailing assistance and support.

Tengku Datuk Dr Zainal Adlin, Chairman, and Ms Irene Benggon Chararuks, General Manager of Sabah Tourism Promotion Corporation, for their valuable support.

Datuk Joseph Guntavid, Director of Sabah Museum, for permission to use photographs from the Woolley Collection. Mr Clement Lee (Borneo Divers), Mr Desmond Hatton, Ms Regina Sulit (Rasa Ria Resort), Ms Monica Chung (Nexus Resort Karambunai), Mr Wembley Mogindol (Sipadan Dive Centre), Mr Ken Chung, Ms Veronica Lee (Pulau Sipadan Dive Resort), Ms Victoria Hilley (Sutera Harbour Resort), Mr David Goh (Mantanani Island Resort), Ms Wong Seu Lin (Sabah Air), Ms Noredah Othman, Ms Alice Yap and Mr Edmond Jokinin (Sabah Tourism Promotion Corporation) for assistance in sourcing photographs.

Dr Wong Khoon Meng of the University of Malaya, Kuala Lumpur, and Ms Anthea Phillipps, for advice in the initial stages of the project.

Ms Patricia Regis (Ministry of Tourism, Environment, Science and Technology, Sabah), Dr Geoffrey Davidson (WWF Malaysia), Mr Peter Malim (Wildlife Department) Ms Stella Moo-Tan (Sabah Museum), for editorial advice.

Dr Heng Aik Cheng, for lending historical material. Drs Hans P. Hazebroek, for preparing the map of Sabah. Mr Christopher Hanson-Smith, for permission to use bird paintings by the late Commander Hughes. The Sabah Society kindly consented the reproduction of a photograph from *Kinabalu—Summit of Borneo*. Thanks are also due to Mr Cheng Jen Wai for computer assistance.

INDEX

(Compiled by Cheng Jen Wai)

Page numbers in bold indicate illustrations.

Titles published by Natural History Publications (Borneo)

For more information, please contact us at

Natural History Publications (Borneo) Sdn. Bhd.

A913, 9th Floor, Phase 1, Wisma Merdeka

P.O. Box 15566, 88864 Kota Kinabalu, Sabah, Malaysia

Tel: 088-233098 Fax: 088-240768 e-mail: chewlun@tm.net.my

www.nhpborneo.com

Head Hunting and the Magang Ceremony in Sabah by Peter R. Phelan

A Botanist in Borneo: Hugh Low's Sarawak Journals, 1844–1846 (Edited and introduced by R.H.W. Reece and with notes on Hugh Low's plant portraits by P.J. Cribb)

Mount Kinabalu: Borneo's Magic Mountain—an introduction to the natural history of one of the world's great natural monuments by K.M. Wong and C.L. Chan

On the Flora of Mount Kinabalu in North Borneo by Otto Stapf. Reprint with an Introduction by John H. Beaman

A Contribution to the Flora and Plant Formations of Mount Kinabalu and the Highlands of British North Borneo by Lilian S. Gibbs. Reprint with an Introduction by John H. Beaman

Discovering Sabah by Wendy Hutton (English, Chinese and Japanese editions)

Enchanted Gardens of Kinabalu: A Borneo Diary by Susan M. Phillipps

A Colour Guide to Kinabalu Park by Susan K. Jacobson

Kinabalu: The Haunted Mountain of Borneo by C.M. Enriquez (Reprint)

National Parks of Sarawak by Hans P. Hazebroek and Abang Kashim Abg. Morshidi

A Walk through the Lowland Rainforest of Sabah by Elaine J.F. Campbell

In Brunei Forests: An Introduction to the Plant Life of Brunei Darussalam (Revised edition) by K.M. Wong

The Larger Fungi of Borneo by David N. Pegler

Rafflesia of the World by Jamili Nais

Pitcher-plants of Borneo by Anthea Phillipps and Anthony Lamb

A Field Guide to the Pitcher Plants of Sabah by Charles Clarke

Nepenthes of Borneo by Charles Clarke

Nepenthes of Sumatra and Peninsular Malaysia by Charles Clarke

The Plants of Mount Kinabalu 3: Gymnosperms and Non-orchid Monocotyledons
  by John H. Beaman and Reed S. Beaman

The Plants of Mount Kinabalu 4: Dicotyledon Families Acanthaceae to Lythraceae
  by John H. Beaman, Christiane Anderson and Reed S. Beaman

Slipper Orchids of Borneo by Phillip Cribb

The Genus Paphiopedilum (Second edition) by Phillip Cribb

The Genus Pleione (Second Edition) by Phillip Cribb and Ian Butterfield

Orchids of Sarawak by Teofila E. Beaman, Jeffrey J. Wood, Reed S. Beaman and John H. Beaman

Orchids of Sumatra by J.B. Comber

Dendrochilum of Borneo by J.J. Wood

The Genus Coelogyne: A Synopsis by Dudley Clayton

Gingers of Peninsular Malaysia and Singapore by K. Larsen, H. Ibrahim, S.H. Khaw and L.G. Saw

Mosses and Liverworts of Mount Kinabalu
  by Jan P. Frahm, Wolfgang Frey, Harald Kürschner and Mario Manzel

Birds of Mount Kinabalu, Borneo by Geoffrey W.H. Davison

The Birds of Borneo (Fourth edition) by Bertram E. Smythies (Revised by Geoffrey W.H. Davison)

The Birds of Burma (Fourth edition) by Bertram E. Smythies (Revised by Bertram E. Smythies)

Swiftlets of Borneo: Builders of Edible Nests by Lim Chan Koon and Earl of Cranbrook

Proboscis Monkeys of Borneo by Elizabeth L. Bennett and Francis Gombek

The Natural History of Orang-utan by Elizabeth L. Bennett

A Field Guide to the Frogs of Borneo by Robert F. Inger and Robert B. Stuebing

A Field Guide to the Snakes of Borneo by Robert B. Stuebing and Robert F. Inger

Man-eating Crocodiles of Borneo by James Ritchie with Johnson Jong

Turtles of Borneo and Peninsular Malaysia by Lim Boo Liat and Indraneil Das

The Natural History of Amphibians and Reptiles in Sabah by Robert F. Inger and Tan Fui Lian

An Introduction to the Amphibians and Reptiles of Tropical Asia by Indraneil Das

Marine Food Fishes and Fisheries of Sabah by Chin Phui Kong

Layang Layang: A Drop in the Ocean by Nicolas Pilcher, Steve Oakley and Ghazally Ismail

Phasmids of Borneo by Philip E. Bragg

The Dragon of Kinabalu and other Borneo Stories by Owen Rutter (Reprint)

A Cultural Heritage of North Borneo: Animal Tales of Sabah by P.S. Shim

Land Below the Wind by Agnes N. Keith (Reprint)

Three Came Home by Agnes N. Keith (Reprint)

White Man Returns by Agnes N. Keith (Reprint)

Forest Life and Adventures in the Malay Archipelago by Eric Mjöberg (Reprint)

A Naturalist in Borneo by Robert W.C. Shelford (Reprint)

Twenty Years in Borneo by Charles Bruce (Reprint)

With the Wild Men of Borneo by Elizabeth Mershon (Reprint)

Kadazan Folklore (Compiled and edited by Rita Lasimbang)

A Cultural Heritage of North Borneo—Animal Tales by P.S. Shim

An Introduction to the Traditional Costumes of Sabah (eds. Rita Lasimbang and Stella Moo-Tan)

Bahasa Malaysia titles:

Manual latihan pemuliharaan dan penyelidikan hidupan liar di lapangan
oleh Alan Rabinowitz (Translated by Maryati Mohamed)

Etnobotani oleh Gary J. Martin (Translated by Maryati Mohamed)

Panduan Lapangan Katak-Katak Borneo oleh R.F. Inger dan R.B. Stuebing

Other titles available through
Natural History Publications (Borneo)

The Bamboos of Sabah by Soejatmi Dransfield

The Morphology, Anatomy, Biology and Classification of Peninsular Malaysian Bamboos by K.M. Wong

Orchids of Borneo Vol. 1 by C.L. Chan, A. Lamb, P.S. Shim and J.J. Wood

Orchids of Borneo Vol. 2 by Jaap J. Vermeulen

Orchids of Borneo Vol. 3 by Jeffrey J. Wood

Orchids of Java by J.B. Comber

Forests and Trees of Brunei Darussalam (eds. K.M. Wong and A.S. Kamariah)

A Field Guide to the Mammals of Borneo by Junaidi Payne and Charles M. Francis

Pocket Guide to the Birds of Borneo Compiled by Charles M. Francis

Kinabalu: Summit of Borneo (eds. K.M. Wong and A. Phillipps)

Ants of Sabah by Arthur Y.C. Chung

Traditional Stone and Wood Monuments of Sabah by Peter Phelan

Borneo: The Stealer of Hearts by Oscar Cooke (Reprint)

Maliau Basin Scientific Expedition (eds. Maryati Mohamed, Waidi Sinun, Ann Anton, Mohd. Noh Dalimin and Abdul-Hamid Ahmad)

Tabin Scientific Expedition (eds. Maryati Mohamed, Mahedi Andau, Mohd. Nor Dalimin and Titol Peter Malim)

Klias-Binsulok Scientific Expedition (eds. Maryati Mohamed, Mashitah Yusoff and Sining Unchi)

Traditional Cuisines of Sabah (ed. Rita Lasimbang)

Cultures, Costumes and Traditions of Sabah, Malaysia: An Introduction

Tamparuli Tamu: A Sabah Market by Tina Rimmer